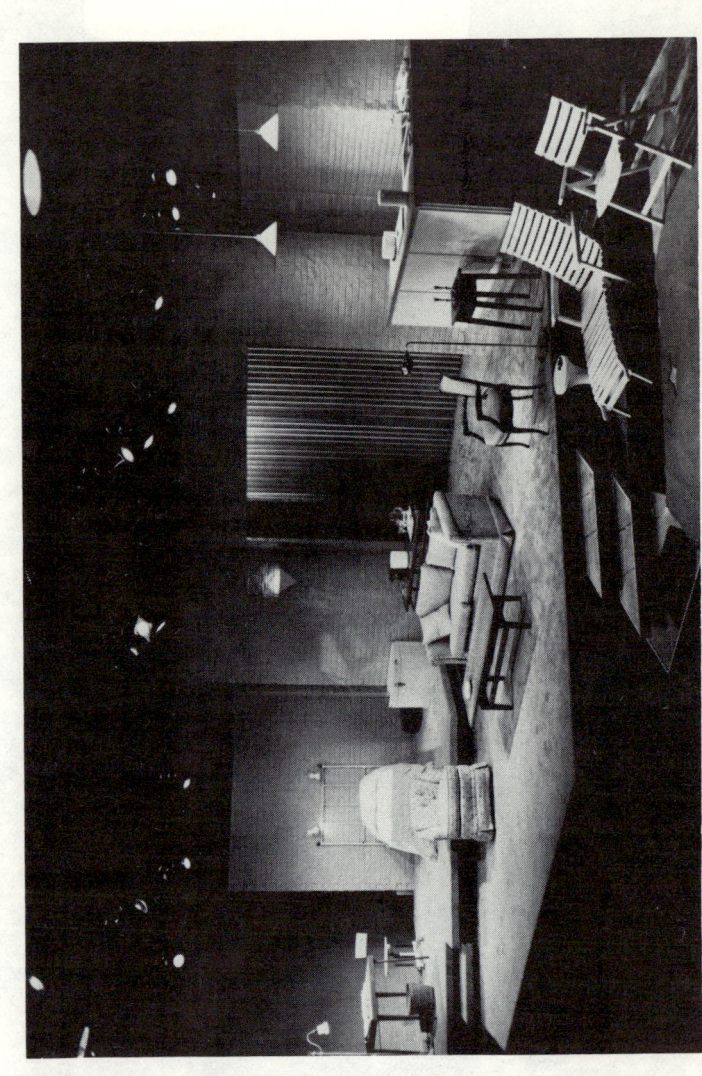

Photo by Gerry Goodstein

Set for the Circle Repertory Company production of "Domestic Issues." Designed by David Potts.

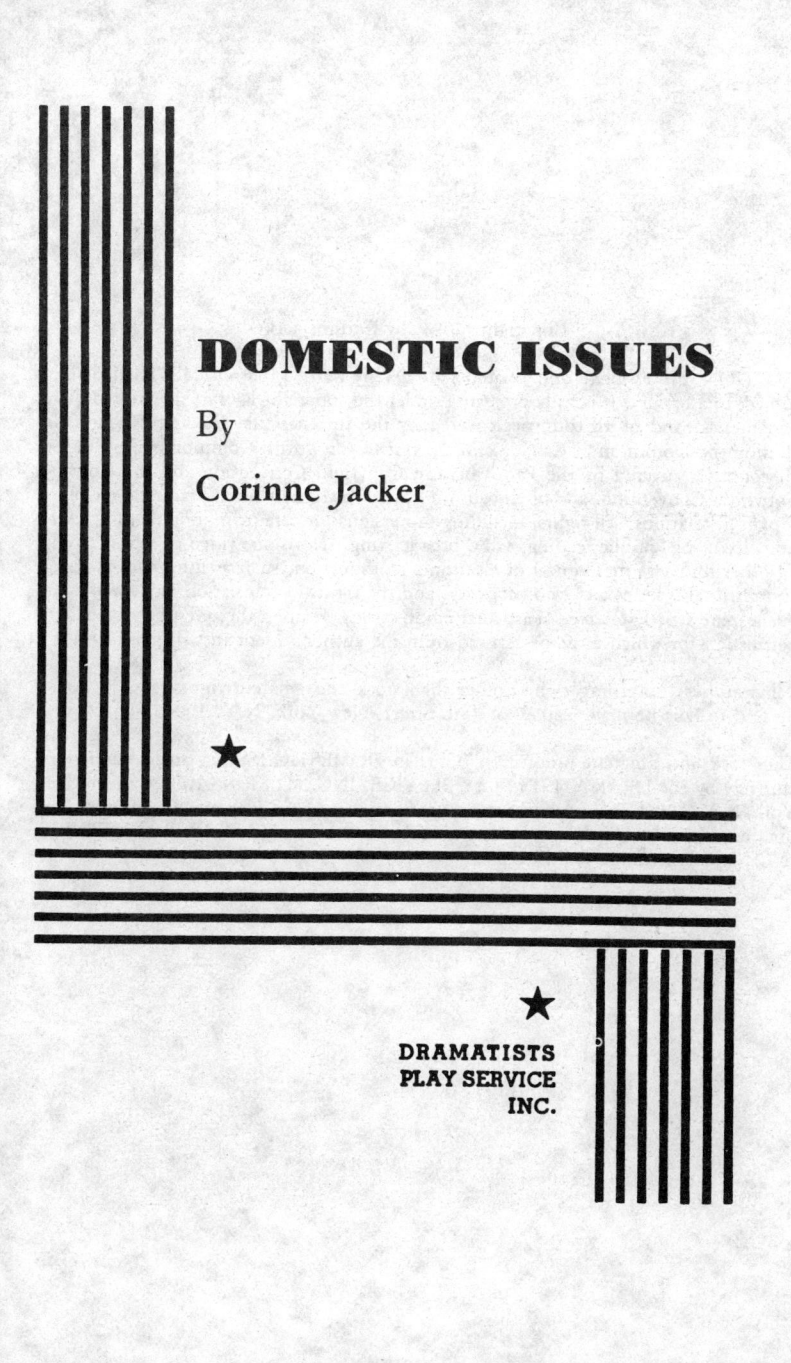

DOMESTIC ISSUES

By

Corinne Jacker

DRAMATISTS
PLAY SERVICE
INC.

© Copyright, 1983, by Corinne Jacker

CAUTION: Professionals and amateurs are hereby warned that DOMESTIC ISSUES is subject to a royalty. It is fully protected under the copyright laws of the United States of America, and of all countries covered by the International Copyright Union (including the Dominion of Canada and the rest of the British Commonwealth), and of all countries covered by the Pan-American Copyright Convention and the Universal Copyright Convention, and of all countries with which the United States has reciprocal copyright relations. All rights, including professional, amateur, motion picture, recitation, lecturing, public reading, radio broadcasting, television, video or sound taping, all other forms of mechanical or electronic reproduction, such as information storage and retrieval systems and photocopying, and the rights of translation into foreign languages, are strictly reserved. Particular emphasis is laid upon the question of readings, permission for which must be secured from the author's agent in writing.

All inquiries concerning rights (other than stock and amateur rights) should be addressed to Lois Berman, 240 West 44th Street, New York, N.Y. 10036.

The stock and amateur production rights in DOMESTIC ISSUES are controlled exclusively by the DRAMATISTS PLAY SERVICE, INC., 440 Park Avenue South, New York, N.Y. 10016. No stock or amateur performance of the play may be given without obtaining in advance the written permission of the DRAMATISTS PLAY SERVICE, INC., and paying the requisite fee.

The World Premiere of DOMESTIC ISSUES was part of the Winterfest program at Yale Repertory Theatre. It was directed by Barnet Kellman; the setting was by Michael H. Yeargan; the lighting was by Michael H. Baumgarten; costumes were by Dunya Ramicova; stage manager was Shannon J. Sumpter. The play opened January 10, 1981.

CAST
(In order of appearance)

STEVE PORTER	*Nicolas Surovy*
NANCY GRAHAM	*Gina Franz*
LARRY PORTER	*Daniel Gold*
SUSAN PORTER	*Marcia Jean Kurtz*
ELLEN PORTER	*Ellen Parker*
GEORGE ALLISON	*Dann Florek*

The first production of DOMESTIC ISSUES in New York City was at Circle Repertory Company. It was directed by Eve Merriam; the setting was by David Potts; the lighting was by Dennis Parichy; costumes were by Joan E. Weiss; sound by Chuck London and Stewart Werner; company stage manager was Jody Boese. The play opened March 2, 1983.

CAST
(In order of appearance)

SUE PORTER	*Joyce Reehling Christopher*
LARRY PORTER	*Robert Stattel*
STEVE PORTER	*Michael Ayr*
NANCY GRAHAM	*Glynnis O'Connor*
GEORGE ALLISON	*James Pickens*
ELLEN PORTER	*Caroline Cava*

TIME AND PLACE

A Friday evening in early September, this year, at Larry and Sue Porter's home in suburban Chicago.

DOMESTIC ISSUES

ACT I

We are in various rooms in Larry Porter's large and expensive home in suburban Chicago. There is a living room—well furnished, tidy, but neither ostentatious nor intimidating. Sliding doors lead to a patio, which has some fancy outdoor furniture. Past the patio is the beginning of a well-cared for and [out of our sight] very large lawn.

The rest of what we see consists of part of a kitchen, where most of the family meals are eaten, and a section of the downstairs bedroom, which is being used by Stephen Porter, Larry's brother. Out of sight on the main floor are the dining room, a small powder room, and a flight of stairs that leads up to the second floor where Larry and his wife, Sue, have their bedroom. Two more rooms await the Porters' kids when they come home for a visit; there are also two full bathrooms upstairs.

During the play, the life of the house always goes on. People are in different rooms, doing different things—eating, sleeping, dressing, talking. They have no more and no less privacy than they would have in any home.

The lights, as they intensify and dim, form the pattern of the action that the audience is to follow. When the people come into light, they are usually in midaction. What they do goes on before the lights bring them to our attention and afterwards as well.

It is late afternoon, a hot Friday in early September, a hot, Indian summer kind of day. Nancy Graham, a writer in her mid 20s, is working at the card table that has been set up in the bedroom as a makeshift desk. She has a pile of papers, a typewriter, notebook, pens and pencils, etc. She is going over a draft of a manuscript in progress, using a marker liberally to cross out whole sections.

Larry Porter is on a step stool in the living room, hanging streamers of crepe paper in anticipation of the celebration of his brother Steve's birthday.

Sue Porter, Larry's wife, is just finishing preparations to begin blessing the sabbath candles.

Steve, Larry's brother, is in the living room, lighting a cigarette, watching Larry putting up the decorations.

Time: The present.

SUE. (*Quietly, almost under breath.*) Baruch atoh adonoi elohainu me'elech holem. Asher kiddishonu bemitzvotsove vitsivonu, l'hadlich ner shel shabos.
LARRY. (*From atop the ladder.*) Good shabos.
SUE. Good shabos. (*She looks at Steve who goes on smoking, apparently oblivious.*)
LARRY. Good shabos, Steve.
STEVE. (*Not aggressively.*) Yeah.

SUE. Sometimes I wonder why I bother with the lights. I'm the only observant Jew left in this house.
LARRY. You got enough religion. You could make a minyan all by yourself.
STEVE. Decorations look terrific, bro.
LARRY. I'm trying to make up for lost time. You haven't been here for the last dozen birthdays.
SUE. *(To Steve.)* You know how he is about occasions. . . . And you should quit smoking.
STEVE. Been a long time since I could afford a good cigarette.
LARRY. Hey, Steve, I got a good one for you. . . . How many scientists does it take to screw in—
SUE. *(Cuts him off.)* Don't let him start. Ever since you've been back he can't stop with all the jokes he's heard since you left. He's a lunatic. Unfortunately for me, he is also kind, generous, lovable, good—
LARRY. Sexy.
SUE. Sexy. Exactly my trouble. One look from you and I dissolve—like yeast with sugar all over it.
LARRY. I am giving you the benefit of the doubt and assuming that was a compliment. *(In the bedroom, Nancy begins typing her revisions. Steve hears the typing as it starts. Larry has finished with the streamers and gets off the step stool. Larry, to Steve, about the decorations.)* So, you approve?
STEVE. Very Colorful. . . . Pink and orange.
LARRY. Yeah! Decorator colors.
SUE. *(Giving Steve a hug.)* He's so tickled you're home. *(And she goes back to the kitchen to continue her work on the canapes.)*
STEVE. You didn't have to do all this shit.
LARRY. Humor me. *(Larry goes to the bar, where he has put a gift-wrapped package.)* Happy birthday, schmuck!
STEVE. Thanks. *(He puts the package down on the coffee table and sits on the sofa. Sue has put a few canapes on a*

plate and takes them in to Nancy.)
LARRY. So—open it. (*Steve nods, begins to undo the paper, ribbon.*)
NANCY. (*To Sue, who is handing her the plate.*) Thanks. (*Sue samples one.*) Fantastic!
LARRY. Like it used to be! This present alone. Just between the two of us.
STEVE. (*A little edgy.*) Like when I was a kid.
LARRY. You're still the kid to me.
SUE. (*To Nancy.*) How's it going?
NANCY. Okay. Slow. . . . He doesn't like talking about it all.
SUE. I don't blame him. I'm just glad it's over. . . . You think it's over?
NANCY. I don't suppose he'd've come back if it weren't. (*Steve has the package open. It is a Polaroid camera, with flash attachment, and several packs of film.*)
STEVE. Hey, bro, thanks.
LARRY. It's okay. (*Steve gets to work putting the camera in order, attaches the flash, puts in the film, etc. Stops, puts the camera down, gets up, awkwardly hugs Larry.*)
STEVE. You son of a gun! (*They are uncomfortable, but both feel a real love for one another. In the bedroom, Nancy takes another canape. Steve goes back to putting the camera together.*)
NANCY. I don't know how you have the patience to make all this stuff.
SUE. I have a good time. (*Sue takes the plate from Nancy and sits on the bed.*)
LARRY. (*About the camera.*) You like it?
STEVE. Yeah. It's great.
LARRY. They modernized it a lot the last coupla years. Nice little toy.
STEVE. Yeah. That's very important to us kids.
SUE. I used to make all the fancy stuff for my mother's parties. She could do all the basic cooking, you know. But she

couldn't make it look good. So she sent me down to Dennisons—they had this course in centerpieces, making stuff like turkeys and brides and place cards to go with. . . . Her favorite was this thing I found in Better Homes and Gardens once—penguins made out of hard boiled eggs and black olives. . . . (*She demonstrates to Nancy.*) You take a toothpick and make one olive the head, and then you cut another one in half for the flippers or the wing things, whatever they're called, and then you make buttons, they stick on automatically. And there it is—a penguin. From then on, from the time I was then, for the high holidays every year I had to make my penguins. (*Steve takes a picture of Larry.*)
STEVE. Gotcha! (*He removes the picture and prepares to take another of Larry.*)
LARRY. (*Waving his hand over the ashtray.*) You smoke too much. (*Steve picks up the cigarette and takes another drag.*)
STEVE. Yeah. You're right. I do. (*He takes another picture of Larry.*)
LARRY. You always were a stubborn son of a bitch.
STEVE. So you used to tell me.
LARRY. We're glad you came home, Stevie.
STEVE. Yeah. Well, I'm lucky I had a rich brother who could buy me back.
LARRY. I called in a few markers, that's all.
STEVE. You don't get somebody an amnesty by calling a few markers—
LARRY. I told you to forget it! You don't want to know all the details.
STEVE. Yes I do.
LARRY. Come on, Steve! . . . You talk like you were public enemy number one.
STEVE. I was on the list.
LARRY. And you aren't now.
STEVE. Why not?
SUE. I brought these in here for you not for me. (*She gives*

the plate to Nancy.)
LARRY. Some people owed me. What the hell, I'm somebody around here.
STEVE. Heshey Goldman said you're the biggest contractor in Chicago.
LARRY. In the midwest.... Where'd you meet him?
STEVE. Around.... In India. He was at an airport, so was I. We had a cup of coffee.
LARRY. Heshey isn't a part of it? —
STEVE. Of what I was doing? Hell, no. He was on a tour — to see the Taj Mahal. (*Steve takes another photo of Larry.*)
LARRY. So. I run a big company. I know some politicians. I helped some get elected, and so on and so on.
STEVE. And you told them I was deballed now and it was safe to let me come home.
LARRY. Will you stop? It's your birthday. Give me a break, will you? (*Larry hits Steve with a throw pillow from the sofa. Steve hits back with the other pillow. They stop after a couple of hits, laughing.*)
STEVE. I'll pay you back. (*Nancy starts typing in the bedroom.*)
LARRY. You came back. You're forgetting all that shit. That's payment enough ... Hey, you hear about the frog who went to the bank for a loan?
STEVE. Later, Larr.... You hear that typing going on? She'll have my ass if I don't get back to work. (*He picks up the camera and instructions.*)
LARRY. Don't let her pressure you. You've only been back a few weeks. You need to settle in, make friends. Maybe find a place for you and Ellen.
STEVE. Ellen isn't coming back.
LARRY. She might. People change. You did.
STEVE. You think so?
SUE. (*Sue stands, picks up the plate from the floor where Nancy had put it, places it on the card table and heads for*

the living room.) I better check that chicken I've got in the oven.
LARRY. (*Sees Sue as she enters the living room. He stops her as she goes by.*) Okay, you don't want a place of your own. You stay here. We're lonely since the kids left for school. And Sue can't learn how to cook for just two—
STEVE. Shut up, will you, Larry? You made your point. (*He heads for the bedroom but Larry stops him.*)
LARRY. Speaking of points. This frog was concerned about interest rates, so he went to the bank and he asked about a loan.
STEVE. See you later, bro. (*He makes a fast exit to the bedroom, Larry folds up the step stool and goes into the kitchen. (Steve, to Nancy.*) How's it coming? (*He stands beside her, rubbing her back. Nancy pushes his arm away.*)
NANCY. Not now. I'm into something.
STEVE. Yeah. (*He goes to the bed with the camera.*)
SUE. (*To Larry as he sneaks a canape.*) What are you doing?
LARRY. A couple. That's all I'm taking.
SUE. Get out of my kitchen!
LARRY. I have an ulcer. I'm supposed to have a snack.
SUE. Don't give me *buba meises*. Take what you stole from me and get out! (*Larry puts the stool away, then settles down to watch her. In the bedroom, Steve simply won't be brushed away. He is once more trying to make a play for Nancy.*)
NANCY. Steve!
STEVE. It's my birthday.
NANCY. Which would you rather be—fucked or famous?
STEVE. (*As he settles into Nancy's chair with her.*) Both! Simultaneously.
NANCY. The ecstasy would drive you mad.
STEVE. (*Indicating the canapes.*) Have a little nourishment. It'll make my sister-in-law happy. She says you're too thin.
NANCY. The hell she does.
STEVE. I thought every female wants to be told she's too thin.

NANCY. Can you just shut up long enough to read my revision? (*Steve nods, she hands him a few pages. In the kitchen, Sue is finishing up the canapes.*)
LARRY. That's enough already.
SUE. Unnhhhhh-hunnnnh.
LARRY. He liked his present.
SUE. He's lucky he's got you for a brother, you know that?
LARRY. I was thinking today at the office, about how different he was. When he was a kid, you know. Never did anything the least bit out of line. No dope. No drinking. He was this straight-arrow kid.
SUE. That's good. You have any idea what he's got on his mind now?
LARRY. He's never been the sort who confides.
SUE. You could ask a couple of questions. (*Larry shrugs, Sue resumes preparing appetizers. In the bedroom, Steve has finished reading. He hands the papers back to Nancy.*)
STEVE. It's good.
NANCY. It's too vague. You don't tell lies exactly, you just don't tell the whole truth.
STEVE. About what?
NANCY. About Steiner. Did you kneecap him?
STEVE. Not me personally. I told you he was kneecapped.
NANCY. In Buenos Aires.
STEVE. In a suburb.
NANCY. Who did it? (*Steve shrugs.*) But you know it was done.
STEVE. Yeah. I know it was done. (*Steve sits on the bed, looks at the camera instructions. She leaves him alone. In the kitchen, Sue decides to have another try at talking to Larry.*)
SUE. I'm asking what's going on? Steve sits there. He smiles. He eats a good meal. But what's he got going on in his head? Why'd he decide to come back all of a sudden?
LARRY. He wanted to come home.
SUE. Sure he did. And what's next? We have two boys— your sons. They're coming home next weekend from school.

Now if he's making bombs in the basement or something, maybe you should know about it before the kids walk in the front door.
LARRY. Why didn't you talk like this before I got him the amnesty?
NANCY. Steve—we are going to have to get into the hard questions.
STEVE. Okay. We make a fresh start tomorrow and I'll really get down to it.
NANCY. Starting today, please. . . .
SUE. Who knows who's sitting across the alley right now with a telescope looking into my kitchen.
LARRY. Don't mock me. All right? (*Larry is feeling the stirring of his ulcer acting up. He gets a Di-Gel.*)
NANCY. You worried about what's going to happen? After your people find out about the book?
SUE. FBI, CIA, PLO? Maybe there's somebody from the South Chicago Liberation Front out there.
STEVE. Nobody's going to be worried about what I tell you. I'm not valuable any more. And I'm not giving out the kind of secrets they want kept. You think anybody's going to buy a book that lists all the safe houses in Guatemala. They changed it all anyway day after I flew back here.
SUE. I keep feeling like a bullet's right around the corner. . . . I look under the hood of the car every day before I go to the market.
LARRY. You see the way he looks now? Ten pounds heavier, twice as strong as he was a month ago. He's settling down. You've got to quit being a Jewish mother with him. Hey! That reminds me. How is a Jewish mother like 60 Minutes?
SUE. I give up? How?
LARRY. (*Making a clicking sound, like tsk-tsk or the ticking clock on 60 Minutes.*) Tkkk-tkkk-tkkk-tkkk. (*Sue hugs Larry who then goes into the living room and begins to mix up a pitcher of martinis. Sue sets about clearing away the dirty*

dishes, fills the sink with soapy water.)
NANCY. Your people did more than kneecapping?
STEVE. They're not my people! . . .
NANCY. People died?
STEVE. I suppose.
NANCY. You don't know?
STEVE. I wasn't there. I was not in the front lines. Not after a while. . . . I was more efficient if I concentrated on the material.
NANCY. But you knew?
STEVE. Yeah. I suppose. I knew it could happen. Sure. People got hurt. You take a package you put it in the post office and then you get out of there. You don't want to see who's there. You don't want to see who got hurt. Jesus! Only a sadist would hang around and count the crowd. And I didn't even take the packages.
NANCY. You were very distant.
STEVE. Everyone has a job to do.
NANCY. Is that why you left the movement? (*Allison suddenly appears in the bedroom. It is clear that he is not entering the room as a living person would. Nancy, of course, does not perceive his entrance. But Steve is always aware of him.*)
ALLISON. Nobody ever leaves the movement.
STEVE. (*To Nancy.*) Guy I knew, George Allison, told me nobody ever leaves the movement.
NANCY. You haven't mentioned him.
STEVE. He's dead. He was my friend.
NANCY. How'd he die?
STEVE. He blew up. In Paris.
ALLISON. Nobody ever leaves the movement. When you die, they bury it with you.
NANCY. He was your friend. What did you think about that? (*Steve again tries to hide by starting something with Nancy.*)
STEVE. How come I don't turn you on?

NANCY. You do. What did you feel about Allison?
STEVE. I dunno. . . . People I talked to about it, it was just words. A lot of rhetoric. I don't talk rhetoric any more.
ALLISON. I'll teach you all over again, man.
STEVE. Nobody sets out to do stuff. I mean, you don't wake up when you're six and say hey, I want to grow up and start a revolution.
NANCY. So when did you decide?
STEVE. When I had to.
NANCY. You weren't poor, you weren't black, you weren't oppressed. Why'd you stay with it?
STEVE. We had the time. We had the knowledge. We had the opportunity.
ALLISON. You either oppress or you fight for the oppressed.
STEVE. Okay. That's it. No more today. . . . Listen, Nan, you want to quit, it's okay with me.
NANCY. Who said anything about quitting?
ALLISON. What do you think everybody's doing? Ellen, Maury, those stupid Frenchies. Hey, Steve, why don't you tell her how I taught you tactics? . . . You remember that morning before we totaled the lab at Michigan State? You were fussing over the stuff like an old lady. I thought if I had to wait ten more minutes I'd lose my guts. And all you did was sit there with the stuff in your hands like you were Michelangelo.
STEVE. (*To Nancy.*) What're you writing? (*No answer.*)
ALLISON. You weren't going to let us go anywhere until you got it right.
STEVE. You know what it feels like—watching you type out my life like it was a steno exercise?
ALLISON. You always needed to get it just right. (*Steve rips the page out of the typewriter, crumples it up and throws it away.*)
NANCY. Hey! That was mine.

STEVE. Property is theft. In this society, if it's a question of human life or property, it's human life that always goes down.
NANCY. I thought you'd given rhetoric up.
STEVE. Don't fucking try to bait me.
NANCY. I'm not playing games, Steve.
STEVE. What do you want? The sugar and honey about how I wanted to save the world? Sure. That's how it was. We were going to turn American around. Allison would give this speech about how we were going to get the boys out of Nam, and win the civil rights battle, and he would have you ready to bust out crying. And it worked. We got out of Nam, and we got blacks into middle management, and everybody went back to sleep.
ALLISON. Only one way to wake people up. You make a big bang.
STEVE. Okay! We were dumb. We thought what we did mattered.
ALLISON. Don't give me that! It matters. You remember all that publicity about the lab.
STEVE. Okay, babe. You want the gory details. I'll tell you about the Honeywell lab.
NANCY. (*Makes a dive for her notebook.*) Just a sec.
STEVE. I don't think you're gonna approve.
NANCY. I don't have to approve. Oriana Fallaci doesn't approve of all the people she writes about.
STEVE. The kid wants to be Oriana Fallaci okay. We had this do-it-yourself Napalm.
NANCY. How'd you figure out how to make it?
STEVE. An army manual. It wasn't hard. Two parts gasolene to one part soap flakes. It's supposed to be a jelly, but we just left it liquid. It worked fine.
ALLISON. Yeah. Real fine.
STEVE. We didn't know how much to use. One of the guys—Andy Moscowitz—he was a real klutz. We used to kid

him about it. He was pouring the stuff on computer cards and some must've gotten on his trousers. Nobody noticed. Probably he didn't either. And, see, Andy was trying to get in. Nobody really wanted him on the scene, you know.
ALLISON. Christ, it was a mess.
STEVE. So when he touched the room, he lit himself up, too. He didn't even have the brains to roll on the floor or anything. He didn't want to scream because he didn't want the guards to hear him, so he ran out, flaming like a comet. By the time we saw him and got the fire extinguished—it smelled like a barbecue, you know. And his clothes were sticking to him. He couldn't sit. He couldn't lie down. We stood around him and we were crying and finally somebody volunteered to call the cops, and Andy propped himself against a wall and waited. He wouldn't let anybody stay with him.
NANCY. And you left him alone?
ALLISON. We had to get to a meeting.
STEVE. He was okay.
NANCY. Suppose he hadn't been.
ALLISON. Then he wouldn't have been. We clean up our own messes.
NANCY. How did you feel, afterwards?
STEVE. I was sorry for him. He fucked up his chance to be a part of things.
NANCY. And you went on to bigger and better adventures.
STEVE. I learned how to make safer materials. Good gadgets that you could trust. (*He takes a piece of paper and sketches out a simple bomb for Nancy.*) Elementary physics. That's all you need.
NANCY. And the will to do it.
STEVE. You know what happened to Andy Moscowitz? . . . After he got out of the hospital, he had to exercise a lot, and swim, to get his muscle tone back. He liked it. So he went back to school. And he teaches P.E. now, at

Deerfield Academy. (*Steve works on the sketch for a few moments more.*)
ALLISON. Those were the best times. At the beginning. When you could see it so clearly. The enemy. Right in your sights.
STEVE. (*He hands the sketch to Nancy.*) There you go. You want to try one? I'll give you a list of materials.
NANCY. (*Flatly, but honestly.*) If I could go out and blow something up, I wouldn't be a writer, would I?
ALLISON. Sabotage is a tool. (*Steve picks up the camera, begins to snap pictures of her.*)
NANCY. Stop it, please.
ALLISON. Put the camera away, Steve. (*He takes another picture.*)
NANCY. I don't like having my picture taken.
STEVE. You blow up a department store, you say something about the goods that are in the store and what people will give up to have them. (*He takes another picture.*)
NANCY. Please. I'm serious. (*She holds her hands over her face.*)
STEVE. (*Camera ready.*) Okay, Nan. I'm sorry. (*She lets her hands down, he snaps a picture.*)
NANCY. Damn you.
ALLISON. What're you doing, playing with toys? Why'd you come back here?
STEVE. My brother just gave it to me. For my birthday. He wants to keep me amused.
NANCY. I don't want my picture taken. Not ever.
STEVE. (*Gives her the Polaroid print.*) Afraid of what you'll see?
ALLISON. You gotta stop trying to do it their way, Stevie.
STEVE. He's got my best interests at heart. Larry bought me amnesty and paid my way home, and now he's paying for a hobby—
NANCY. What about your wife? She's still underground.

STEVE. You don't ask about my wife! . . . (*To Nancy.*) I'm sorry.
NANCY. . . . I'm touchy about having my picture taken — (*A silence.*) Was it one of these that went off in Paris? Your friend, Allison, was he in Paris?
STEVE. . . . Yeah. In Neuilly.
ALLISON. Nobody's holding it against you.
STEVE. That wasn't my responsibility.
NANCY. A bomb you are putting together goes off when you aren't in the building and you don't feel responsible?
STEVE. Allison shouldn't have tried to mess with it.
ALLISON. Somebody had to finish the damn thing.
STEVE. He didn't know shit about technical issues. . . . We were trying to make the gadget because somebody needed it. . . . We were helping — what the hell. I can't expect you to understand.
NANCY. I get angry. My father gets angry. We don't go out on the street with guns.
STEVE. They send military aid to El Salvador, that should have started a revolution. They torture people in Argentina, what do you do about it?
NANCY. There are legal ways — sanctions, economic penalties, we can withhold ordnance. What do you want to go around blowing things up for?
STEVE. (*Interrupting her before she finishes.*) It's all about power! . . . Maybe you need a lesson in power. Come here. (*He yanks her toward him, kisses her, hard. She tries to resist.*) I'm bigger than you are. I'm stronger. When you turn away from me, like you did before. I get mad.
NANCY. Steve!
STEVE. So I've got you in here and I'm telling you shut up or I'll do something worse. Get out of your clothes. (*He throws her on the bed.*)
NANCY. Come on, Steve.
STEVE. You know I mean it. Because you humiliated me.

You made me mad. I'm gonna rape you. What're gonna do, Nan? (*He kisses her again, hard. Larry has been drinking martinis, has dozed off. Ellen, Steve's wife comes in to the living room from the patio.*) You understand more now?
NANCY. You'd do it?
ALLISON. If he had to. (*Steve releases her. Nancy goes to her chair at the card table. Steve removes his shirt and starts to put on his dress shirt from the head of the bed.*)
ELLEN. Hi, Larry. Where's the birthday boy?
LARRY. (*Jerks awake.*) Jesus!
ELLEN. I figured I didn't have to ring the bell.
LARRY. Did he know you were coming?
ELLEN. I wanted it to be a surprise.
LARRY. He's in the downstairs bedroom. I'll get him.
ELLEN. I'll do it. (*She goes to the bedroom. Larry heads for the kitchen. Steve is buttoning his shirt as Ellen walks right into the bedroom.*) Stevie. Happy birthday. (*They embrace.*)
LARRY. Ellen's here. She walked right in. Just now.
SUE. Here?
LARRY. I'm telling you. (*Sue starts to head for the bedroom; Larry stops her and leads her back to the kitchen.*)
STEVE. I don't think anybody was expecting you, Ell.
ELLEN. I know.
STEVE. . . . You want to use the john or anything? Nancy,—this is my wife, Ellen. You want to get her a towel or anything? . . . Come on into the living room, then, babe, okay?
ELLEN. Sure. (*He finds the martinis in the living room and pours himself a drink. Nancy stops Ellen in the bedroom.*)
NANCY. I'm Nancy Graham.
ELLEN. I know where to find the towels.
NANCY. I'm writing the book with Steve. We use this as our office—
ELLEN. . . . He wrote me about you. About the book. . . . You look like you'd be a good fuck. (*She walks into the living room, leaving Nancy who sits down, makes*

more notes.) Happy birthday, husband.
STEVE. You said that already.
SUE. So? What do we do about it?
LARRY. Ask if she wants a sandwich.
SUE. Was he surprised when he saw her?
LARRY. I wasn't there.
SUE. If he was surprised, it could be all right. Then he wasn't expecting her.
LARRY. She's his wife.
SUE. You didn't buy her any amnesty.
LARRY. She didn't want one.
SUE. That's what I mean.
ELLEN. Why did you walk out on me?
STEVE. Back then or just now?
LARRY. You never liked her.
SUE. She's wanted by the F.B.I.
LARRY. Maybe she changed her mind, like he did.
SUE. Sure and the cow jumped over the moon . . . Suppose she was followed here?
ELLEN. I would have let you know, Maury thought it wasn't safe.
LARRY. It's after five o'clock on Friday night. Who am I supposed to call? Hello, 911, my sister-in-law the revolutionary just turned up.
SUE. If anything funny happens, you're obligated to call someone. If she's here she wants something.
LARRY. Just because she wants it, doesn't mean he'll give it to her. (*Steve and Ellen are now seated on the sofa.*)
STEVE. What's up? How'd you get in?
ELLEN. Mexico. Maury fixed it . . .
STEVE. Maury fixed it?
ELLEN. He knew I wanted to be with you on your birthday.
STEVE. What's up?
ELLEN. We can talk about it later. You look good. . . . Your skin's cleared up. (*In the kitchen, Larry digs his hands into the soapy water, comes up with bubbles, water dripping.*

He squirts some at Sue who squirts some back at him.
LARRY. Okay! It's war! (*He goes after her, hands full of soap bubbles.*)
SUE. I give up!
LARRY. Not till I get you! (*The game gets a little more physical.*)
SUE. Come on! I have to check the chicken!
LARRY. Chicken yourself!
SUE. That's enough! Quit it!
LARRY. Not when I'm ahead. (*He gets another handful, pushes it in her face. It gets in her nose and mouth, and Sue begins to cough. Larry pulls back.*) You okay, baby?
SUE. Let me be. (*During this, Nancy has come into the living room.*)
NANCY. Do you want to be alone?
ELLEN. Why?
NANCY. I'm sorry—
STEVE. Wait a minute. I thought you wanted to understand the movement. (*Indicating Ellen.*) You are looking at the Rosa Luxemburg of the 1980's.
NANCY. Please. Don't try to make a fool of me.
STEVE. And don't be contemptuous of my wife!
ELLEN. (*Affectionately.*) Shut up, Stevie.
STEVE. I thought you had more guts than that? What're you worried about? At this moment the house is surrounded by 12 members of the Red Brigades. Anybody tries to get in or out— (*He makes a motion of slashing his throat.*)
NANCY. You don't have to settle for me. Find another ghost writer.
STEVE. For which she is being paid $20,000 and 10% of my gross in perpetuity. Not bad for a kid her age, is it?
NANCY. You're not doing so badly either—for a reformed revolutionary.
ELLEN. Who says he's reformed?
NANCY. He came back here, didn't he?

ELLEN. So did I, didn't I?
NANCY. *(To Steve.)* Aren't you?
STEVE. *(To Ellen.)* Am I?
ELLEN. *(To Nancy.)* Is he?
NANCY. I've been wondering myself.
STEVE. What's new, Ell? Who's in? Who's out?
ELLEN. It's all the same.
STEVE. Sure it is. *(Steve gets up to go into the bedroom where he will load the camera with a new film cartridge and get the camera.)*
ALLISON. Tactics, man. *(Allison exits.)*
NANCY. He wasn't expecting you, was he?
ELLEN. I wanted to give him his present in person.
NANCY. So what's he doing back here?
ELLEN. *(After a moment.)* Yo no se.
NANCY. It'd hurt Larry a lot — to find out he's being used.
ELLEN. Everybody uses everybody, don't they?
NANCY. Don't ask me. I just work here. *(Steve comes back, sees the two women still together in the living room, picks up his drink and goes off by himself onto the patio. Ellen picks up her purse and starts to head for the patio.)* Steve talks about power.
ELLEN. Yes.
NANCY. Is that why you do it?
ELLEN. Whatever you want to call it. *(Ellen goes out onto the patio. Larry enters from upstairs, having changed for dinner.)*
LARRY. *(To Nancy.)* How's it going, kiddo?
NANCY. Ca marche. *(Nancy goes back to the bedroom, begins working on the manuscript. Larry pokes his head out the patio door to talk to Steve.)*
LARRY. What do you think? White or red wine with the chicken?
STEVE. Was it male or female? *(Larry laughs, goes to the kitchen.)*

LARRY. So, how do I look? This okay?
SUE. You look fine. Now go in and make the living room look fine for me.
LARRY. Will do. (*Larry goes into the living room, he picks up the camera box, ribbon, empties the ashtray and returns to the kitchen. Out on the patio, Ellen and Steve are sitting quietly. It is dark by now. The crickets are loud and insistent.*)
ELLEN. Suburban crickets sound different.
STEVE. That's because they're well fed. (*He takes the camera, snaps a picture of her.*)
ELLEN. You buy that with your spending money?
STEVE. Birthday present from my bro.
ELLEN. Terrific. I wish I had a dress—you know, not the shmates I wear.
STEVE. We'll get you one tomorrow.
ELLEN. I don't have any money.
STEVE. I do. (*He takes out some money, large bills, pulls several off the wad.*)
ELLEN. Yeah.
STEVE. . . . My prize for being co-opted. (*Ellen shakes her head.*) Come on. Take advantage of the capitalists. Go to Saks. Have your hair cut. Buy some underwear.
ELLEN. (*She takes the money, puts it in her pocket.*) You keep looking at her tits.
STEVE. I like looking. I used to look at yours all the time.
ELLEN. Used to. (*Steve takes another picture.*)
STEVE. Gotcha!
ELLEN. You gonna be a photographer when you grow up?
STEVE. I haven't gone to bed with her, you know.
ELLEN. I didn't think you had.
STEVE. (*He takes another picture.*) Thanks.
ELLEN. You're welcome. (*Ellen has taken each picture as it has been taken. She puts them into her purse and removes a small package. Larry is jumpy and edgy, worried about Sue's silence, Ellen's return. He pinches Sue on her behind.*)

24

SUE. Cut it out!
LARRY. So how many psychiatrists does it take to change a light bulb?
SUE. Freudian or Jungian? And is it during therapy?
LARRY. Come on!
SUE. I give up—how many psychiatrists does it take to change a light bulb?
LARRY. One. But it really has to want to change.
ELLEN. (*She hands Steve the package.*) Happy birthday, love. (*He takes it, opens it, pulls out a chain with a silver medallion on it, large, beautiful, clearly, old and hand made.*)
STEVE. Wow!
ELLEN. Anna helped me get it. She knew a guy who collected the stuff.
STEVE. How's Anna?
ELLEN. (*Coldly, shrugs.*) I dunno. Haven't seen her for a while, couple weeks.
STEVE. . . . Sure. . . . I'm no longer on the privileged list. No classified information for Stevie.
ELLEN. You left.
STEVE. I had to.
ELLEN. You didn't have to come this far.
STEVE. I thought I did.
ELLEN. You didn't ask me if I wanted to go along.
STEVE. I knew the answer.
ELLEN. . . . I kept expecting you back.
STEVE. It wasn't anything personal, Ell—
ELLEN. Oh.
STEVE. I missed you.
ELLEN. I was right there, where you left me.
STEVE. I couldn't come back.
ELLEN. There are always ways in and out. . . . Didn't you want to come back?
STEVE. Yeah. . . . Sometimes.
ELLEN. You don't have to worry, I don't come begging,

Steve. I wait, but I don't beg.
STEVE. Come on, Ell.
ELLEN. It wasn't just the store blowing up.
STEVE. I couldn't face you after that. That's the truth.
ELLEN. You know the trouble with you—you can't tell the truth. Almost, but not quite. Don't be scared. Your family needs you, Stevie. Maury needs you. We need you.
STEVE. Ellie. Oh, God. I dunno—
ELLEN. Stevie. Hey, Stevie. . . . (*She holds out her arms, he goes to her, they embrace. She is very tender, very loving. She puts the medallion around Steve's neck. He will pick up his camera and drink and go back to the living room. Ellen will put out his cigarette, pick up her purse and follow Steve into the living room. In the kitchen, Larry has been drinking from the milk container.*)
LARRY. That all the milk we have?
SUE. You're going to be sick again.
LARRY. I got a twinge—
SUE. You got an ulcer symptom. . . . You'll be in the hospital. Transfusion, special diets—scare me and the kids to death. Very sensible.
LARRY. I felt like a glass of milk. Don't make a federal case out of it.
SUE. . . . You better talk to both of them.
LARRY. I talk to Steve all the time.
SUE. You have to find out what's up.
LARRY. Absolutely! And then he'll have a good excuse not to confide in me. That's what happened the last time. She'll use it against us. . . . He'll talk if he wants to talk. In the meantime, stop worrying and get the cake decorated. We're having a birthday party.— (*Silence. Sue steps out of her shoes.*)
SUE. I can't wear heels any more. My feet are too old. (*She goes off to get the cake and icing.*)
ELLEN. I have this absolutely definite feeling that you wanted something and I didn't give it to you. What?

STEVE. After what happened—after Allison—I came to you didn't I?
ELLEN. And?
STEVE. My God—we must've stayed in bed three, four days. In that heat.
ELLEN. (*Grins.*) I made you take your salt pills.
STEVE. Yeah. I remember. I never sweat so much in my life. Then, all of a sudden, I went dry. It could be 105 and I wouldn't sweat a cupfull.
ELLEN. I failed you.
STEVE. No. You were terrific, but when you talked about the world, I kept worrying about losing us, and then—when you talked about us, or kissed me, or—I couldn't stop thinking about the world.
ELLEN. Steve, I don't sleep at night because you aren't there to wrap myself around. You stay here and you'll dry up, clean and sanitary and tucked in at night with Gladwrap over your head. You went dry because you lost your vision. Don't blame it on me.
STEVE. And I'm going to get it back by making more stuff to blow things up?
ELLEN. What happened in Neuilly wasn't your fault. Allison messed up. He didn't know what he was doing.
STEVE. So he died.
ALLISON. (*As he appears in the living room.*) So what?
STEVE. (*To drown him out.*) So I'm no good now. My hands shake. My heart isn't in it. I could make another mistake.
ALLISON. Don't blame it on me, Stevie, you being scared. You want my blessing, you've got it.
ELLEN. It's time to call Maury.
STEVE. You can't use Larry's.
ELLEN. It's okay. The phone's clean. They still got that extension upstairs? Come on.
STEVE. Ellie— (*He picks up the camera.*) Hey! You know where the word snapshot comes from? George Allison told me. The old English hunters used to go out in Africa and it

was a code of honor—You saw the game, and you took the gun, like this— (*He takes the camera.*) and—snap! The shot's off without even aiming it. The gentleman's way. Your arm takes the recoil, and if you know what you're doing, the leopard or whatever is dead.
ALLISON. Brilliant, absolutely brilliant!
ELLEN. Maury's waiting.
ALLISON. Deadeye dick.
STEVE. You do this one, okay?
ELLEN. Okay. This one. (*She goes upstairs to make the call.*)
ALLISON. You fired after you had any hope of hitting him.
STEVE. I have a lousy sense of timing.
ALLISON. Nicked him in the heel maybe.
STEVE. I'll get the hang of it.
ALLISON. I doubt it. You fire late because you don't want to hit the bastard. Even when he's imaginary. You take the gun and you go through the arc, almost any place at all, you're going to hit something vital. (*He demonstrates, making an arc with his arm, firing when the gun would be dead on target.*) Gun out, one motion, arm moves, you shoot. Get it?
STEVE. If I wanted to learn how to shoot, I could have joined ROTC.
ALLISON. If you're afraid of damaging anyone, you should get out now. The movement doesn't need sensitive people.
STEVE. Jesus!
ALLISON. Okay. You're a brain. You know which wire to put where. Guy's like me just oil the wheels. But we're the ones who safe up the territory so your little genius boxes can be put in place.
STEVE. It's not necessary.
ALLISON. We don't decide what's necessary. We do it. If it has to be done.
STEVE. Hey, man, I may be ready to drop out, but I'm sure as hell not ready to take anyone out.
ALLISON. The hell you're not. You make bombs.

STEVE. Which are supposed to go off when no one is in the area.
ALLISON. And if someone gets there—by mistake or miscalculation or general fuck up?
STEVE. It's an accident.
ALLISON. Sure. It isn't murder because you didn't plan it?
STEVE. I'm not a murderer.
ALLISON. Bullshit. The hell you're not. You should wear blinders all the time then, man. Because someday maybe I'll be the enemy, or Ellen, or Maury. And then what. We won't be unknown soldiers, will we?
STEVE. When you become the enemy, I'll kill you.
ALLISON. Terrific. Pick up your gun. I said pick up your gun. You don't pick up your gun, you bastard you're dead right now. (*Steve hesitates.*) One of us is going to fire. You've got a count of five.
STEVE. Stop playing games with me.
ALLISON. This is no fucking game. You shoot me or you are dead. (*Allison undoes the snap on his holster.*) One-two-three—
STEVE. Do what the hell you want. I'm not playing.
ALLISON. What kind of revolution are you in, Porter? (*Steve does not answer.*) You going to give up putting your little explosives together for us?
STEVE. I'm in until I decide I'm out.
NANCY. (*Comes in from the bedroom.*) Listen, if we're going on with the book, whatever you've got planned now has to be in it.
ALLISON. Either we're going to tangle or you're gonna turn into the weirdest kind of buddy I ever had.
STEVE. Revolutions make strange buddies.
NANCY. (*Taking the remark as addressed to her.*) You have my word. I won't tell anyone anything till you give me permission.
STEVE. Suppose we were going to put a bomb in the Pentagon? Or the White House?

NANCY. Is that it?
STEVE. Or some nice well-to-do little suburb. You still wouldn't try to stop us?
NANCY. Is that what you're going to do?
STEVE. It would be a statement. . . .
ELLEN. (*Stops at the entrance to the room for a moment.*) Steve—Maury says hello. (*She goes into the kitchen where Larry is working with Sue. Ellen heads for the coffee pot.*)
LARRY. Hey, Ellie! Use a sentence with the word "tamale" in it? Come on, Ellie,—tamale.
ELLEN. I like enchiladas better than tamales.
LARRY. Wrong!
ELLEN. So? What's right?
SUE. (*After prompting from Larry.*) The sun wasn't hot to Jake, but it sure was hot tamale.
LARRY. Get it? Hot tamale. Hot to Molly.
SUE. She got it.
ELLEN. I got it.
LARRY. (*To Ellen.*) We're gonna go this winter. All the way down to the tip of South America. (*Larry feels another pain, and then another, quickly.*) Be right back. (*He goes to the bathroom.*)
NANCY. That's a nice medallion.
STEVE. Ellen gave it to me.
NANCY. I didn't know it was your birthday. . . . Before I got here—
STEVE. That's okay.
ELLEN. Nice cake. . . . Steve likes a fuss. Even when he says otherwise, you know.
SUE. We know.
NANCY. Are you going to leave with her?
STEVE. Maybe she'll stay here with me.
NANCY. Do you want to stay? (*No answer.*) If you're still in it, you have to go, don't you?
SUE. (*In the kitchen still, with Ellen.*) Larry went out on a limb, getting Steve. . . . He owes some important people—

ELLEN. He told them Steve reformed?
SUE. Have you?
ELLEN. My politics are none of your business.
SUE. Politics? The kindest thing I can say about the things you did before you left—
ELLEN. And since. . . . We kept busy the last twelve years. You mention Steve in places where it counts and you'll find out he's famous. He's a hero.
SUE. Not to me. Not to a lot of people.
NANCY. Are you going to do it? With her?
STEVE. You ask too many fucking questions.
NANCY. That's my job.
ELLEN. You won't get into any trouble about me. Nobody knows I'm here.
NANCY. When I said I'd write about you, I thought there was one big difference between us. Commitment. I don't have to write the book, you know. I can quit tomorrow. But you—I thought you had to do it—what you did. . . . Do you?
ELLEN. I just have to stay the night. Is that all right with you?
NANCY. Are you afraid people won't agree with you? That they'll say you were wrong? You shouldn't have done what you did?
ELLEN. I don't want to make any trouble. I had to see Steve, that's all.
SUE. What happens if you get caught? (*Ellen shrugs.*)
ELLEN. Why should I?
SUE. How do you stand it?
ELLEN. Nothing much ever gets to me.
SUE. Me either. (*They smile at one another.*)
NANCY. That's one of the techniques of brain-washing, isn't it? Enforced silence.
SUE. What's it like? When they pick you up—the police.
ELLEN. Depends on the country. . . . It's always tense. . . . Like this.

31

NANCY. That's what you're doing, isn't it? Trying to make me uncomfortable? Feeling guilty?
ELLEN. After the interrogation starts, it's easier. . . . The unknown. That's the hard part.
NANCY. Shrinks do it, too.
ELLEN. So. Do I stay or go? . . . I'd like some time with him. . . .
NANCY. They sit there and listen and don't answer.
SUE. Stay.
NANCY. Okay. It's working. I feel guilty. What'm I supposed to feel so guilty about. Do *you* feel guilty? Because you walked away from people who counted on you? Because of what you did when you were in the movement? Because you can't stay and you can't go?
STEVE. No more today, okay? The office is closed. (*Ellen hears the last of Steve's words.*)
NANCY. Aha! Score one for Ms. Nancy Graham.
STEVE. (*To Larry on his way back to the kitchen from upstairs.*) The kid is indefatigable.
ELLEN. What's he been telling you just now?
NANCY. Nothing. It's like trying to get Yuri Andropov to unbutton.
LARRY. (*In the kitchen, to Sue.*) So when do we eat? I'm starving.
SUE. Ten minutes.
ELLEN. (*To Nancy.*) But I interrupted?
NANCY. Right.
LARRY. You look like hell, Sue. What's up?
SUE. Nothing.
STEVE. (*Sensing the sexual tension.*) Maybe I should go outside.
ELLEN. Fix me a drink.
STEVE. (*To Nancy.*) That means you're getting to her.
ELLEN. Not her.
STEVE. What, Maury? What'd he say?
LARRY. She been after you?

SUE. We talked, that's all.
NANCY. Who's Maury?
STEVE. Ask Ellen.
NANCY. Is he your—what do you call it, chairman? Leader?
STEVE. Ell knows what he is, don't you, Ell.
ELLEN. Okay. I'll make my own drink.
NANCY. Don't talk to each other in code because I'm here.
LARRY. We have ten minutes? You go upstairs. I'll watch things down here.
SUE. I'm fine.
LARRY. Just go upstairs and wash your face and put some perfume on, will you? Trust me. I can take care of things.
NANCY. Would you like the children to leave the room?
ELLEN. (*Politely.*) Would you like a drink? (*Sue stops in the living room on her way upstairs.*)
SUE. Everything okay? . . . We eat in ten minutes.
NANCY. That's what my parents did. When I was a kid. Talk to one another at dinner, right over my head. In French. Some power play. (*Larry settles on a stool, but he is exhausted. He leans back, closes his eyes, drifts off into a light sleep.*)
STEVE. (*To Ellen.*) You okay?
ELLEN. Yeah. I haven't had a martini in a long time. I forgot.
STEVE. Take it easy. They're meant to be sipped.
ELLEN. . . . I don't know. It's that damn kitchen. All those neat white cabinets filled with cans of salmon and tuna fish. And the frig. I looked in the frig. Steak. This enormous T-bone. Made me jealous because I won't be here to eat it. Appliances. . . . I couldn't figure out what half of them do. Like I was on the starship Enterprise.
NANCY. So are you going to let me be one of the grownups?
ELLEN. That's your choice.
NANCY. You've got something planned.

ELLEN. I'm his wife, not Mata Hari.
NANCY. You came back because you've got an operation going. And Maury's part of it, and you and Steve. What kind of action is it? (*Ellen sips her drink.*) Okay. Just tell me about it. As an observer.
ELLEN. We don't have observers.
NANCY. Don't you want a sympathetic eye? Someone to write it up for the media.
ELLEN. We've been made fools of enough.
NANCY. Or do you keep it secret just to pretend it's important.
STEVE. Hey, Nan, you ever wonder why the women in the movement carry such big purses.
NANCY. What's she got in there?
STEVE. And she never lets it out of her sight.
NANCY. What's in there.
STEVE. She had an assignment tonight.
ELLEN. (*Assuming he will talk about Maury.*) No more, Steve.
STEVE. Why not? Nan wants a piece of it. Let her have it. . . . The bag's got a small explosive device. Big enough to make a noise, but nothing to do any real damage.
NANCY. Why?
STEVE. So it'll look like Maury and the rest are after me. Because I'm talking to you. Then, when I disappear, the last place any one's going to look for me is with them.
NANCY. (*To Ellen.*) Is he telling the truth?
ELLEN. . . . No.
NANCY. I've had it with you and your fancy little fraternity with the secret codes and the special handshakes. I was a damn fool for taking you seriously. (*She takes her note pad, goes out onto the patio, tries to relax.*)
STEVE. Don't look at me like that. I know I was being shitty.
ELLEN. It comes with the territory.
STEVE. And don't forgive me. (*Larry wakes up, looks*

around him. He feels awful, gets out a Di-Gel, goes for milk.) It's not so damn easy, Ell. Try spending a month with you folks.
ELLEN. I wouldn't.
STEVE. Oh yeah, dinner with Paul and Marge. . . . You gonna call?
ELLEN. It wouldn't be a terrific idea.
STEVE. I guess not.
ELLEN. . . . I thought about it.
STEVE. Sure.
ELLEN. You telling me I should?
STEVE. Come here, babe. (*He takes her in his arms, and for once they can have a simple little kiss, not full of anything but love and sexual attraction. As they are beginning to enjoy it, Sue comes through the archway from upstairs on her way to the kitchen.*)
SUE. . . . You can wash up before dinner, if you want to. (*She goes to the kitchen, where she catches Larry with is Di-Gel.*) I knew it.
ELLEN. (*Laughing.*) I forgot. Places like this have rooms, but no privacy. . . . (*Nancy, who has been unable to relax, comes in from the patio, goes to the bar and pours herself a martini.*)
NANCY. Yes dammit. I'm still writing the book. I'm one hell of a stubborn woman. (*She goes back to the patio.*)
LARRY. I feel lousy.
SUE. You're not as young as you were twelve years ago.
LARRY. I thought I was smarter, though. (*Allison has entered the living room, when he enters Steve stands and moves away from Ellen.*)
ELLEN. Go on out there, if you want to go.
ALLISON. Listen to this. (*He reads from his notebook.*) "In order to get rid of the gun, it is necessary to take up the gun. The revolutionary carries out his action."
ELLEN. Steve?
ALLISON. "One, two, a thousand lives are not important."

ELLEN. You okay? (*Ellen has gone over to Steve, concerned.*)
STEVE. Don't hover, Ell. I'm fine.
ELLEN. Sure. . . . Come and get me if you need me. (*She takes her purse and goes into the kitchen.*)
ALLISON. Did you hear me, Steve.
SUE. (*To Ellen, as she comes into the kitchen.*) You want to help? You can clean the beans. (*Larry feels a real twinge.*) You're going to the doctor tomorrow.
LARRY. If I've only got a couple weeks left, at least let me go out with a joke. What's Irish and stays out all summer? — Patio furniture. (*Larry has another twinge. Ellen fishes through her purse. Allison exits the living room, leaving Steve alone.*)
SUE. (*To Larry.*) Go lie down.
LARRY. Before dinner? (*Ellen takes out a bottle. She gets a pill.*)
SUE. (*To Ellen.*) What is it?
ELLEN. I've got a headache.
SUE. What do you take?
ELLEN. I don't know. They help the pain.
SUE. You shouldn't take pills unless you know what they are.
ELLEN. A doctor gave it to me.
SUE. They're supposed to put the ingredients on the bottle.
ELLEN. I took a lot. Nothing happened to me.
SUE. If it was that good, you should write him and —
ELLEN. I don't know his name.
SUE. Oh.
ELLEN. It's no big deal. I got shot once. I was in Milan. You don't ask for references in a case like that.
LARRY. How did it happen?
ELLEN. I was running from a cop. . . . Actually, I was escaping from prison. It was supposed to be all arranged. But this cop didn't seem to know about it.
LARRY. What'd you do?

ELLEN. I left a package.
LARRY. What kind of package?
SUE. A bomb.
ELLEN. It went off. Nobody got hurt. But they caught me.
SUE. Anybody ever get hurt from one of your packages?
ELLEN. A couple of times. (*She grabs her purse, leaves, goes to the living room. To Steve:*) We need to talk.
STEVE. Not now.
ELLEN. We don't have time.
STEVE. It'll have to wait. (*Steve retreats to the bedroom. Ellen stays in the living room. As Steve enters the bedroom, Allison appears in the bedroom. He is carrying a bomb.*)
ALLISON. You know what I'd do. If they asked me for a target. I'd total Mt. Rushmore. George Washington—Blam! Thomas Jefferson—Blam! Who else? Oh yeah, Teddy Roosevelt—Blam! Don't try to cop out on me, man. Guys like you, they lose interest once there are no big moral issues to fight for. You can't admit the bomb's enough. All by itself.
STEVE. Not for me.
ALLISON. Don't give me that. You can see it in a guy once he's smelled the blood. I killed—you killed.
STEVE. (*Furious.*) Get the hell off my back!
ALLISON. I love you, man, like you're my brother. I'm trying to help. It doesn't do any good to walk away from the power. It just waits, getting bigger and bigger. Eventually, either you eat it or it eats you.
STEVE. You don't own me anymore.
ALLISON. You scared, Stevie? Because my bomb's real? Just like all the real ones you made before.
SUE. (*To Larry.*) She admitted it. She has blown people up.
LARRY. She exaggerated. To shock you. Like using dirty words.
SUE. I'm completely dizzy with all the things I don't know. What happens if we don't call anyone?
LARRY. Will you please leave it alone?

SUE. And suppose tomorrow or the next day we read about people getting hurt. It could be our fault.
LARRY. One thing at a time. Let's have some dinner. You get something in your stomach, you'll be less upset.
SUE. I let the chicken burn.
LARRY. That's okay. We've still got the cake. You hear the one about the PLO terrorist who tried to blow up a bus? . . . He burned his lips on the exhaust pipe. I guess that was in bad taste. (*Ellen has finally gone into the bedroom to Steve.*)
ELLEN. Have you thought about it?
STEVE. I don't know—
ELLEN. It won't be easier later.
SUE. (*To Larry.*) Use lots of candles, it makes the cake look bigger.
ALLISON. (*About the bomb he's examining.*) I think I'm figuring it out.
ELLEN. You can do it. I know you can.
STEVE. What? What is it he needs me for?
ALLISON. Jesus! All the different colored wire and all!
STEVE. If I don't go with you, Ell, I can't stay here, right?
ALLISON. Hey! You changed something. The wiring isn't like the drawing shows.
ELLEN. We'll do it together. Like in the old days.
STEVE. A long time ago.
ALLISON. You ever read Dan Berrigan, Steve? Father Berrigan? Someone came to Father Berrigan and asked him how he knew what he was doing was a true revolutionary act or not—
ELLEN. You have to make up your mind tonight.
STEVE. They trust me enough to leave me here if I say no?
ELLEN. I'm holding my arms out to you. I'm asking you to put away your toys and come with me.
ALLISON. So this guy asked if he knew what he was doing was a true revolutionary act. Berrigan looked at the guy and

answered: There's never any doubt about the action. I do what I can't not do.
ELLEN. (*As she and Steve embrace.*) I knew you would.
LARRY. (*Lighting the candles.*) It's gonna look like the Chicago fire.
ELLEN. Oh, God, you and me.
ALLISON. One more turn of the screw. You and me.
ELLEN. We've still got it. I can feel it.
LARRY. Okay let's go! (*He and Sue take the cake into the living room, where they turn out the lights.*)
ELLEN. We can do anything that has to be done.
LARRY. (*Yells.*) Hey! Steve! Ellen! Nancy! (*Nancy comes into the living room from the patio. Steve and Ellen separate from their embrace. Ellen goes into the living room, Steve is about to follow.*) Okay, let's hear it now.
LARRY & SUE & NANCY. Happy birthday!
ALLISON. We do what we can't not do. (*He turns the screw. Steve yells.*)
LARRY & SUE & NANCY. Happy birthday!
STEVE. Do it! Damn you! (*There is a blinding flash — as if the bomb had gone off. Every sound stops.*)

END OF ACT I

ACT II

It is a few hours later—about 1 a.m. The remains of Sue's late night snack are out in the living room. Little bits of birthday cake, plates, napkins. The women are in the living room. Sue and Ellen are cleaning up.

In the bedroom, Steve and Larry are sitting together. Larry has a pile of papers, legal documents, business statements that he want's Steve to go over.

SUE. (*To Ellen.*) Why do I feel like any second some big guy in an undershirt is going to kick the front door in and point a submachine gun at me?
ELLEN. There's nobody out there.
SUE. I don't believe you.
ELLEN. Okay. The house is surrounded.
SUE. I don't believe you. How could you come here, put us all in danger?
ELLEN. Because what I do is important.
LARRY. You have any questions? I can answer questions. Nothing's cut and dried. I mean the will, that has to stand, but—
STEVE. I'm really going blotto bro. Can't this wait?
LARRY. You've been putting it off for three weeks now.

STEVE. You can take care of things. I trust you.
LARRY. Trust isn't enough. Things happened in the past few years. You have to understand. Your mother dies, your father dies, there's ten pounds of documents to be taken care of. (*Larry hands him a document.*) Read it. You're not reading it Steve. You're skimming!
NANCY. Do you have people out there?
ELLEN. No one's going to get hurt. Steve and I are leaving soon.
SUE. He's not going with you?
ELLEN. I think he is.
NANCY. What kind of thing are you getting him into?
SUE. Don't take him with you. Get out. By yourself. While nobody's hurt.
LARRY. I don't want to be left with unfinished business.
STEVE. What does that mean?
LARRY. It means are you staying or going?
STEVE. Yeah.
LARRY. Terrific answer, Steve. Very informative.
SUE. Larry and me, we didn't ask to be involved.
ELLEN. You should have.
NANCY. Sue, we aren't going to be hurt. They don't work that way.
SUE. What do you know about it? What you read in the papers, just like me.
ELLEN. Nothing's going to happen to you. And I'm not leaving without him.
SUE. Anyone else want cottage cheese?
ELLEN. Why don't you go to bed? I'll take care of feeding people.
SUE. I'm not sleepy.
ELLEN. You're dead on your feet.
SUE. Why don't you go to sleep?
ELLEN. I'm not tired.
SUE. Okay. I'll go to bed when you do. (*Sue goes to the kit-*

chen, makes tea, gets cottage cheese, puts together a little tray for Larry.)
NANCY. Should she be scared?
ELLEN. We don't make trouble unless we have to.
NANCY. Why didn't you tell her that?
ELLEN. If she's scared she'll be on our side.
NANCY. God, you're tough.
ELLEN. I know the way things work.
STEVE. (*Making another try to get away.*) Listen, Larry, you don't need me to—
LARRY. I say I do need. Before you make any decisions, we're going to get the family business settled . . . Or I make some phone calls. (*Steve gets up, takes his clothes, throws them into a duffel bag.*) Just going to walk out in the middle of the night. I think you owe me more than that. (*Steve continues packing.*) And it's not all on paper. . . . We set dad's stone last year. You haven't seen it. Mom's either.
STEVE. No.
LARRY. Maybe you want to go see them next week—before the holidays.
STEVE. I think I'll skip it, Larry.
LARRY. We go—the whole family, every year. The kids'll be home from school. They'll come with me.
STEVE. I'll be out of the house.
LARRY. I didn't mean *that*. . . . You're not going away with her?
STEVE. My wife is part of my family. . . .
LARRY. You could at least make one trip. Just so you could tell me you approve.
STEVE. I never promised I'd stay forever.
LARRY. You never warned me you'd leave.
SUE. (*As she brings the tea tray into the living room.*) I see the gentlemen are still in the drawing room.
LARRY. Hey, you know, I made promises about you to people. I made certain guarantees.

STEVE. Okay! Come on! I want to get this over with.
SUE. (*Gives a photo album to Nancy.*) Here— (*To Ellen.*) Steve's Bar Mitzvah album . . . And some other pictures you could see after.
LARRY. Can we put the bag away? It's sitting there like a loaded pistol. You know how many times you ran away from home when you were a kid.
STEVE. When I leave here, I'm not going to be running away from home, Larry.
LARRY. Yeah. I know. But hotheaded—you know, you always were hotheaded. I'm telling you you don't have to be. Relax. Take a breath. Find your own way.
STEVE. I came back because I couldn't stay there any more. It's only been three weeks Larry, and I've got my own American Express card, and twenty-five thou from the publisher in the bank. I went looking at cars the other day. I didn't tell anyone, but I went window shopping, and I found one I wanted. And I use your sauna cabinet and your club to go swimming—
LARRY. That's what I'm trying to tell you. There's plenty for it to be yours and mine. . . .
STEVE. I don't know . . . Jesus. This room smells like a tv commercial, fabric softner and air purifiers.
LARRY. You think it's more holy to stink?
NANCY. (*To Sue, holding up a snapshot.*) Who's this?
SUE. Steve, and Larry, and their dad.
NANCY. Larry looks just like his father.
SUE. Yeah—and Steve's the image of the Kahn family. His mother's side. People used to stop him on the street and ask him if he was related to Oscar Kahn. The family's very well known in Chicago.
ELLEN. I'll take that in for you.
SUE. I can do it. (*She heads for the bedroom with the tray. Larry fishes in his pocket for Di-Gel as he talks. Sue enters with the tray in time to see him take the Di-Gel.*)

LARRY. I'm our father's son all right. Soon as I turned forty, the whole digestive system started to go.
SUE. You all right?
LARRY. I'd be better if I had his stomach. Pure cast iron.
SUE. At this time of night, everybody needs a cup of tea. (*She pours the tea.*) Your wife's out there, prowling around like a cat in labor.
STEVE. Be right back.
LARRY. We're not finished.
STEVE. I'll be back. (*He goes to the living room, sees Ellen, goes out to the patio. and she follows.*)
SUE. I found out. She's come to get him all right.
LARRY. Big surprise.
SUE. So what do we do?
LARRY. We try to keep him here.
SUE. What do we do? Handcuff him to the bed?
LARRY. I'm not done talking yet.
ELLEN. We have to leave soon. They'll be waiting.
STEVE. Ell, I'm not sure.
ELLEN. You were a while ago. What did he offer you?
STEVE. You could stay if you wanted to. Larry could fix it.
ELLEN. I'd go crazy in two months. So would you.
STEVE. You get used to it.
ELLEN. How many years did it take us not to get used to it?
STEVE. Maybe it's not so bad.
ELLEN. You're the only one who can do it.
STEVE. What are they going to do?
ELLEN. . . . It's big, Steve.
STEVE. Maury's always doing big things.
ELLEN. Nobody else has even come near this.
STEVE. What's he got? Nitro? Plastic?
ELLEN. No.
STEVE. TNT?
ELLEN. No.
STEVE. Okay! Is it bigger than a breadbox?

ELLEN. It's the biggest.
STEVE. That egomaniac is going to set something off in the United States.
ELLEN. Something manageable.
STEVE. Don't tell me.
ELLEN. The statement cannot be denied.
STEVE. I don't want to hear you.
ELLEN. Someone's going to do it. It should be us.
STEVE. You know?
ELLEN. Steve. (*He goes back to the bedroom, she follows.*) Wait.
LARRY. (*As Steve comes into the bedroom.*) Okay, thanks for the tea, Sue. Now we have to get back to work.
ELLEN. In a minute. Steve—we have an appointment.
LARRY. He owes me five minutes.
ELLEN. It was a swell party, Larry—but he's turned 35 now, and he has to get on with it.
LARRY. Yeah! And he happens to be holding a great future in his hands right this second. You know what I just handed him? It's a partnership agreement. I'm offering my brother 50% of the business.
STEVE. Hey, wait a sec—
ELLEN. You see what happens if you stay? (*She leaves, goes back out to the patio.*)
LARRY. What do you think, Steve. A real Porter family business.
NANCY. (*From the door of the patio, to Ellen.*) What do you think's going to happen, if he goes with you?
ELLEN. He'll do what he has to do.
SUE. (*To Steve.*) Make him eat that. (*Sue goes through the living room and then upstairs.*)
NANCY. Okay. What are your stakes? What's so important to you that you'd blow up the whole world for it?
ELLEN. It's about making something else—community—making a community of communities. Don't try to write that book. You don't understand how Steve works.

NANCY. It's easier than trying to understand you.
ELLEN. Why? I'm simple. I do what has to be done.
NANCY. And we read about another Italian millionaire being kneecapped.
ELLEN. Because we discovered that the power isn't with Mitterand or Thatcher or the Congress of the United States, it's with the Board of Directors of Standard Oil, and Shell, and the Chase-Manhattan. It's the same war. They just wear three-piece suits now and swear allegiance to their balance sheets.
NANCY. It still sounds like rhetoric to me.
ELLEN. It is admitting an action has to be taken.
NANCY. You can't you know. You won't do it. Level the world to the ground and put the men and women back in tents or caves or whatever, you still won't be able to make a race of humans that don't understand the word "I." (*A silence between them. Ellen goes back to the living room. Nancy follows her.*) All any one of us has to do is call somebody and tell them you're here.
ELLEN. That's right. That's all you have to do. You won't because you care about him. You care about individuals. I care about communities.
NANCY. You want him to do this with you because you love him and you don't want to lose him. (*Sue has returned and is standing in the hallway.*)
ELLEN. Sit down, Sue, you might as well wait in a chair. (*Before she sits, Sue gives Nancy another photo album.*)
STEVE. I'm not going to be your partner.
LARRY. I'm not trying to interest you in a hobby.
STEVE. I'm not you're kid sister, you don't have to take care of me.
LARRY. Don't throw this away like you did everything else for God's sake.
SUE. (*To Ellen.*) What're you knitting?
ELLEN. An afghan.
SUE. You do good work.

ELLEN. I've made enough of them. I made mother one. And that one I sent you. And my sister.
NANCY. My mother tried to teach me once—I wouldn't be domesticated.
ELLEN. I wait a lot. It's good to have something to work on while you're waiting. (*Sue nods. Nancy goes back to the pictures. Ellen knits. They are tense, cannot really make conversation easily. Larry is restless. He watches Steve reading, but needs to talk.*)
LARRY. You remember how when you were a kid all you wanted to do was listen to me tell jokes? . . . One after the other, you'd laugh till you couldn't go on laughing any more or you'd split. Why did the moron jump from the top of the Empire State Building?
STEVE. (*With Larry.*) To make a hit on Broadway.
LARRY. A frog goes to the bank for a loan and the officer he talks to says his name is Patrick Whack. Funny name for a banker the frog says. Well, the banker says, I'm Irish. What's your collateral? The frog sighs and says he's only got a little gold monkey, about the size of a thimble. That's no kind of collateral the banker says. It's all I've got, the frog tells him. The banker says he can't authorize a loan with collateral like that. They'll have to see the bank president. The frog agrees. And they go in to see the president. The banker explains that the frog wants a loan. What's his collateral, Mr. Whack, the president asks. And the frog says all he has is a little gold monkey. It's not enough, Whack tells the president. I told him that. Let me see it, the president says, and he holds out his hand. So the frog puts the gold monkey in the president's hand. He looks at it closely. And then he says— (*Larry prepares for the pay-off.*) It's a knick-knack, Paddy Whack, give the frog a loan. (*Larry gets up, feeling queasy. He belches.*) How many radicals does it take to change a lightbulb? Six. One to shoot the landlord and five to picket for a better environment. (*He fishes for more Di-Gel, takes two, sits down, chewing, Steve goes on reading.*)

In the living room, Sue is restless, too, doesn't like the silence.)
NANCY. (*To Sue.*) Whenever I see a woman knitting, I think of layettes.
ELLEN. I've done that, too. Baby sweaters, booties—We had one. A baby girl.
SUE. When?
ELLEN. A long time ago—four years ago.
SUE. Where is she?
ELLEN. She died. Right away. Five days and six hours and seventeen minutes old. Lung congestion. It was a good hospital. The best in Naples. Nobody's fault.
SUE. I wish I'd known.
ELLEN. My theory is that she came out feeling like a foreigner and she couldn't adjust. Charlie—Charlotte, after my grandmother. We should've come back, I guess. . . . But we didn't. . . . You should've seen that hospital—grey walls, mosaic floors, ceilings yea-high, like being in a railroad station.
SUE. Well, they do the best they can—
ELLEN. —You wonder what difference it makes. If she'd lived.
SUE. . . . And you go on? . . . You're the same.
ELLEN. You mean as the last time? Am I? Really the same?
SUE. You make me feel the same—guilty but angry.
ELLEN. (*To Nancy.*) —I came out here—during the Days of Rage.
NANCY. 1969. I was nine years old then.
SUE. She was a mess—Bloody nose. A bump on her head. . . . Remember? She wouldn't stop screaming.
ELLEN. That's the same. I still scream.
SUE. Oh, well, sure. Everybody does. Nobody stops screaming. When the babies come, and when someone dies. The screams just get more inside that's all. Until you don't remember how the sound goes. Now, sometimes, I go into the kitchen and I say to myself "I'm going to scream." And

that's it. That's all I do. I have these recipe cards in colors—
yellow and pink and green, and printed on the top it says
"From the Kitchen of Susan Porter." So, whenever I think up
some fantastic variation on a tuna-noodle casserole I write it
down and pass it on to a friend. And she'll pass me one of
hers. Lentil and sour cream dip, maybe, or tofu lasagna.
NANCY. So why do you go on doing it?
SUE. I don't know how to do anything else. So I go on doing
what I was raised for. I'm the last of an endangered species.
So, whenever I say "I'm going to scream," I take the scream,
and I shove it down the disposall, along with the potato
peels, and I turn on the cold water, and grind it up. Down
the sewer, into a pipe. Off someplace, feeding the baby
alligators. A race of them down there, growing fat on my
screams! It keeps me nice and quiet. (*To Ellen.*) You think
your generation has a corner on anger. Well, see, you don't.
ELLEN. No. My generation's got a corner on action. (*Sue does not reply.*) We're not done talking. I like you. I liked you from the beginning.
SUE. I'm not flattered.
ELLEN. You know why the women are the best—in the movement? . . . Because they can be satisfied just cleaning, just getting rid of the rotten stuff before it spreads. Don't expect a lot of good philosophy from me, Sue. That's Steve's bag. I just want to be able to make one place in the world shining, and clean, and rid of all the garbage. That's enough. Just doing that. I don't need causes and flags and theories. Just down on the floor, on my hands and knees scouring and scrubbing till the flesh on my hands wears away and the blood mixes with the soap water. Don't walk out on me. Don't turn away from me. I know you understand that!
SUE. (*After a moment.*) I've been considering it all, just now. You did—to me, it's terrible things. I told you you could stay. That was a mistake. Please. Don't spend the night here tonight. (*Ellen doesn't answer. She puts on her vest.*)
NANCY. You leaving?

ELLEN. No. (*She sits.*)
STEVE. I know what this means to you but to me it's just money.
LARRY. Sure. Put me down.
STEVE. You expect me to join up. Make a living exploiting a whole class.
LARRY. We employ black people. We employ chicanos. Look at our payroll. Count up the minorities.
STEVE. Affirmative action is a form of exploitation developed by the managerial establishment in Washington.
LARRY. Yeah? It costs me a hell of a lot—training, teaching those people discipline. Some of 'em don't even understand about being on time until you drill it into them.
STEVE. I don't want a nickel from your fascist government.
NANCY. What are you waiting for?
ELLEN. Steve.
LARRY. Laughing at me behind my back. Square Larry who doesn't know the difference between communism and socialism.
STEVE. Bullshit!
LARRY. Yeah. Maybe I'm not an intellectual, but you hear me—I make a hundred and fifty thou a year. And expenses. And I don't pay taxes through the nose like one of your holy liberal saints. You don't even answer me. Too much of an idealist, is that it? Well, what've you done with your morals and your ethics? First it's the Peace Corps and you have this urge to help the world. Then it's my brother the conscientious objector—I'll go to hell before I kill. Then you turn out bombs like jelly beans and you don't give a damn who you kill! You think your father died peacefully? He went to his grave worrying about you. Ashamed of you.
STEVE. Shut up!
LARRY. Even in the hospital at the end, he was asking if there wasn't a word from you. What you do. It doesn't stop with you. It puts a curse on our name, on me, on my kids, on your dead father!

STEVE. So you're going to take me out to the cemetery and show me your pious tombstones. I'll fall on the ground weeping, realize I'll have to get a job and go straight. Your logic is shit, Larry, pure shit.
LARRY. You came back. I figured you were ready to be part of the family again. To carry your weight. Make some decisions for a change instead of leaving it all up to me.
STEVE. You? You make the decisions in his name! How come you never moved into his office? He's dead. The room's empty. Christ! Your office doesn't even have a good view of the street.
LARRY. I'm used to my office. What difference does it make? I run the company now.
STEVE. You run the Edward N. Porter Company. How come he never changed the name? You still worked for dad. What the hell, why not take all the money and put it in a bank account with his name on it. If anyone could figure out how to get money into the next life, it's him! The cheap bastard!
LARRY. (*During Steve's speech, Larry has gone into the living room and torn down the streamers. He then goes out onto the patio. Steve has been following him the whole time.*) You don't talk that way about our father!
STEVE. What? Wasn't he cheap? Didn't he nickel and dime us every minute we lived in his house?
LARRY. I said shut up!
STEVE. You don't tell me to shut up!
LARRY. I'll say what I damn please to you. (*Larry slaps Steve across the face.*)
STEVE. You don't own me!
SUE. (*Sue rushes out onto the patio to Steve.*) LARRY stop that!
LARRY. Get out of here, Sue!
SUE. In our own backyard?
LARRY. I said get the hell out! (*Larry grabs Sue and shoves her back into the living room.*) Go back to your fucking kit-

chen! (*Steve grabs Larry and throws him back onto the patio.*)
STEVE. Hold it!
LARRY. Get out of my way!
STEVE. Make me. (*They fight as Larry tries to move Steve.*)
SUE. Steve!
STEVE. Some fuckin' kid, hunh, Larry? Tougher than you are! (*Steve stops. Larry waits for more fighting, but it doesn't come. He moves painfully. Silence. Larry tries to get his breath back.*)
ELLEN. (*To Sue.*) He'll be all right.
SUE. No. (*She goes to the kitchen.*)
NANCY. (*To Ellen.*) We didn't even try to stop them? (*Ellen sits down in the living room.*)
STEVE. (*To Larry.*) You want to get washed up?
LARRY. In a minute.
STEVE. Did I hurt you?
LARRY. I know what's going on. She came with orders for you, didn't she? Some job for you? They're the ones who own you.
STEVE. Not any more. . . . Maybe it'd be better if they did.
LARRY. Your bag is packed.
STEVE. It always is. . . . What the hell, Larry. If I stayed, it wouldn't mean you were right.
LARRY. My life's okay. . . . (*Larry gets up.*)
STEVE. You shouldn't have let him do it to you—shoving you into the business when you were a kid, apprenticing on summer vacations when you were still in high school.
LARRY. It would've killed him if I'd walked away like you did.
STEVE. He's dead now.
LARRY. You know, what I'd do, if I could—I'd go into labor relations. I'm good at it. And the union guys respect me. I even got invited to Washington one time. To the Department of Labor. There was a panel on setting guidelines for the industry. And they wanted me to be on it. I

would've gone. But we were being audited and I had to stay in town for that.
STEVE. Nobody's stopping you now.
LARRY. I've got responsibilities. Two kids away at school. You know how much that costs?
STEVE. Gauguin was older than you when he went off to the south seas.
LARRY. Yeah. And what'd he get for it? Syphillis. (*A moment. Then they both laugh. Larry leaves. He passes through the living room, Ellen gets up to go to Steve. (Larry to Ellen.)*) He'll be in in a minute. Let him be, all right? (*Larry goes on to the kitchen.*) What's going on here?
SUE. . . . I told her I didn't want her to stay.
LARRY. Susie—the thing between him and me—it goes back a long time farther than that. (*Pause.*) What do we do the rest of the night?
SUE. You have a glass of milk and try to calm down.
LARRY. I'm calm.
SUE. Drink the milk. . . . I love you. (*Steve reenters the living room, Nancy is looking at the photos.*)
NANCY. Family pictures.
STEVE. Put them away, I know what I look like. . . .
NANCY. You look like one of the Kahns.
STEVE. I never told you about our relatives in Germany, did I, Nan? We had a whole bunch of second cousins there during the war—the Second World War. I mean.
NANCY. The Kahn family.
STEVE. Right. My father got a letter in '38. From my mother's Uncle Herman. He wrote about how bad it was and how maybe if my father did something fast they'd be able to get out—a few of them anyway. But you had to guarantee you'd support anyone you brought over. And Dad didn't have that kind of cash. He really didn't even know the German relatives. They were all on my mother's side. . . . You're not taking notes, Nan. We're where you wanted to

be. We're getting the real stuff now. The Hershes down the block brought a nephew over in '37. He turned out to be a gonif and bled them all dry.
NANCY. Your father didn't send the money.
STEVE. Right.
SUE. We can't leave them alone.
LARRY. You want to go in, go in.
STEVE. Herman died. The whole goddam Kahn family died. (*To Larry and Sue, as they enter the living room.*) Come on in. (*They enter and sit down.*) When the war started, and the news of the concentration camps came out, dad felt like hell. He bought war bonds, more than he could afford, and after—money all the time for ORT and Hadassah and Israel. I bet there must be a thousand trees in Israel with my father's name on them.
NANCY. He didn't kill anyone.
STEVE. I'm trying to tell the truth. I hope you're listening to me.
NANCY. Please—I'm a person—. What do you want from me?
STEVE. I'm trying to explain—dad wasn't the only one who felt guilty, was he, Larry? We weren't even born then, but we heard, but we heard the stories. And I was ashamed because I didn't die. You understand me, Nancy?
NANCY. These are family things.
STEVE. I am telling you why I wrote my brother and asked to get me a ticket home and amnesty. More people dying instead of me. In Neuilly. I was alone in Neuilly. Ellen was in Milan then, and I was with the brothers and sisters in Neuilly, making bombs. I was almost done with the device. Just a couple of wires to connect. But it was a fantastic day, and I was restless—I figured the work could wait a half hour. So I went out and bought a bottle of table wine and some cheese and a loaf of bread, and I went to the park, like I was a clerk on my lunch hour, and I ate it all, and drank up the bottle. I didn't hear the explosion. When I got back the street was full

of firemen and cops and the whole neighborhood. The store was blown up. The whole front gone, but you couldn't see in. It was covered with this thick black smoke. Of them all, my good friends who were stuck in small pieces on the store walls, mixed in with the canned tomatoes and fish—the only one who haunts me is Allison—He saw the detonator, almost finished, where I left it.
ELLEN. Don't use him, that's not why you left us.
STEVE. God damn it Ellie, I'm trying to tell you that Allison was my first murder. (*Pause.*) So I left for Kabul. And when I got there, everybody was walking around in the heat and sweating. Even at night, people sweat in their sleep. Things wouldn't get good. I got dysentey. Everything seemed to stink of Neuilly—that charred, burned, acidy-sweet stink of my friends' bodies . . . So I decided to walk to Kandahar. And it was summer, so I could eat stuff I found growing wild, berries and fruit, that kind of stuff. Some days, I stopped and worked for the farmers, mending fences or digging irrigation ditches. I was pretending I was back in the Peace Corps, and they thought it was real cute, a rich American working for food from them. So in this one place, the guy had some work for me and we went out to the fields. And he opened a canvas over the front of his falling-apart shed and there was a spray can, and a hose, and a drum of insecticide, and it said "Product of Dupont Nemours." (*A silence.*) I turned around and walked back to the road. And I walked for a while. Then I sat down. In the middle of the road. I was crying. There was a bus coming at me, but I didn't care. I realized that there was no place I could travel in this world where there would be any uncontaminated life.
SUE. I'm sorry. . . . .
STEVE. The cow patty that was a couple of inches away from me. Even it wasn't pure. Because the grass the cow ate only grew because it had been sprayed with insecticide to kill the fungus and the bugs. Then I realized I was in the middle of the road to Kandahar, crying over a cow patty. I got up, and

I brushed as much dirt off my pants as I could, and I turned around and walked back to Kabul. (*Quiet. They are waiting for more.*) That's it. That was when I figured out that there wasn't going to be any way to help people find purity.
ELLEN. You don't understand.
STEVE. All of a sudden, this thing I'd taken for granted, that I depended on was gone . . . You know how it is when you're driving down the road and you see the tire marks, like when somebody really slams on the brakes, and the tire marks go on for a ways and you can track the car, and then they stop. Maybe there was a crash, maybe not, but the record of the car is gone. So. Wham! I lost it, you know, I lost the faith. All my beautiful rhetoric, all my rationale — gone, like I was naked. And I came back here to be safe, and it's not safe here, either.
NANCY. Are we writing the book together, Steve? Tomorrow, I mean, are we working tomorrow? (*Pause.*) Wait a minute. We know what's going on. Something's going on. And the three of us have agreed that we won't say anything about it, isn't that so? (*Pause.*) I told you I wanted to learn about commitment. Well — oh, God, I am so ashamed to say this — Oh, well, see, it's not for me. Not unless I have to, unless I'm driven to it. I don't know what I'm going to do. Go on writing, sure, but what else. So — (*She laughs.*) I feel like you've detonated me. And it's late. But I want to get in my car and go home. (*To Ellen.*) I'm not going to call the police or anybody.
ELLEN. No. You're not the sort who does.
NANCY. (*To Larry and Sue.*) Goodnight. (*To Steve.*) Goodnight. (*She leaves.*)
SUE. Steve. You came here. That was a promise. Now you think you can break such a promise so easily, and break your brother's heart, too? Okay. Go ahead. My head isn't as big as yours. There's only so much room in my life. If I allow ten people in, I have to push ten people out. We're more important to me, our family, our friends, even you — (*She means*

Ellen.) than all those farmers in Asia and South American and all over. So you go ahead and you blow something up or kidnap somebody, whatever silly thing you've got planned. I'm going to do what's important—stay home, and light the oven, and feed my family. That's what lasts. It's selfish. I know that, Ellen, but that's the way I am. (*She goes upstairs. Larry begins to follow her, but he wants to be with Steve. Yet he can't stay in this room.*)
LARRY. Yeah. Yeah. (*He goes out onto the patio, lies down on the chaise lounge, in a while he falls asleep.*)
ELLEN. They think you're coming with me. You don't have to do it, Steve. You could come along for the ride.
STEVE. No. I couldn't. You think I'm backing out because I can't do it. That's not it, babe. I won't go with you because I can do it.
ELLEN. Oh, God, I don't want to have to go to bed by myself tomorrow night.
STEVE. Me either.
ELLEN. I have to get going in a while, in a couple of minutes. Maury's expecting—me. (*Pause.*) So you'll stay here with her and write the book?
STEVE. No.
ELLEN. No her or no book?
STEVE. Both no. They don't let people just watch here, either.
ELLEN. You can't join up with him?
STEVE. Right now there isn't anything I can't not do. Except leave.
ELLEN. Poor Larry.
STEVE. We shouldn't be in the same place, he and I.
ELLEN. We could go away. To the woods someplace. No tv. No newspapers. You'd build us a house. With your bare hands. We could have a garden. We could become vegetarians and grow all our own food—
STEVE. No we couldn't.
ELLEN. I could.

STEVE. There wouldn't be anyone there to radicalize but the bunnies.
ELLEN. For a while maybe, I could— (*A silence between them.*)
STEVE. How am I going to make it alone?
ELLEN. Don't ask, Steve. Because I would stay. And we'd be miserable. I need you.—I shiver when I hold you. . . . I shiver when I let go of you. I wish somebody was coming to pick me up. That way I'd know how to get away from you.
STEVE. (*After a moment.*) Write me?
ELLEN. Where to?
STEVE. Care of American Express. They'll keep on forwarding it till they find me.
ELLEN. (*With love.*) You idiot. . . . I can't leave.
STEVE. It's okay.
ELLEN. If you say so. (*She leaves very quickly. Steve looks around, he is going to leave. He decides to take only the camera. He is about to leave as Allison suddenly appears.*)
ALLISON. Let's get moving!
STEVE. No more. I was responsible. But I don't owe anybody, Allison. No way. (*He walks out on Allison, leaving him behind.*)
ALLISON. (*Calling after.*) See you around. (*Steve sees Larry lying asleep. It is early dawn, light enough to undo the flash, which he does and snaps a picture of Larry. Then he kisses him gently on the forehead.*)
STEVE. Take care of yourself, bro. (*He leaves.*)

END OF THE PLAY

PROPERTY PLOT

ACT I
BEDROOM

Duffel bag (Under bed.)
Nancy's purse (On back of desk chair.)

On Card Table:
    Typewriter w/ sheet of paper in carriage
    Typewriter pad (under typewriter)
    Pile of typed pages
    Pile of blank typing paper
    Magic Marker
    Pencil
    Box of matches
    Pack of cigarettes
    Ashtray
    Cup of coffee
    Steno pad
    Pen

Waste basket

LIVING ROOM

Ashtray (On coffee table.)
2 throw pillows (On sofa.)

Top of Bar:
   2 "rocks" glasses
   Pitcher of water
   Bar spoon'
   Tray w/ :
      4 martini glasses
      martini pitcher (empty)

Under Bar:
   Bar Mitzvah album
   Bottle of Gin
   Bottle of Vermouth
   Camera in gift package
   Bar towel

Step stool
Streamers hung on archway
Brass tray w/ 2 brass candlesticks (On table stage left.)
2 8" off-white candles (In candlesticks.)

KITCHEN

On top of counter:
   Plate of canapes
   6 sliced cucumbers
   6 pieces of bread
   6 slices of cucumber & bread
   Several toothpicks
   Paring knife
   Teaspoon
   Small cup of parmesan cheese
   Bunch of fresh parsley
   Large plate of cudites
   Damp sponge
   Dish-cleaning brush
   Glass of water

Dish towel
Apron

In sink:
Colander w/ string beans
Small bowl of chopped parsley
Small bowl of radishes
Empty small bowl

Under counter:
1 birthday napkin
Several paper towels
Box of toothpicks
Book of matches

OFFSTAGE UP LEFT (Kitchen.)

Bag of trash
Tea tray w/
5 teacups & saucers
2 spoons
Coffee cup
Cake
3 tubes of cake icing
12 birthday candles in holders
Matches
1 qt. milk w/ small amount of milk
Ice bucket
Small plate (Luncheon-size.)

OFFSTAGE UP RIGHT

Matches
Allison's notepad
Bomb
Diagram of bomb

Screwdriver
Gun in holster
Photo album
Folder w/
  partnership agreement
  trust agreement

PERSONAL PROPS

Stephen:
  $70 bills w/ money clip
cigarette lighter
1 cigarette

Ellen: (In bag.)
  Pills in non-child-proof container
  Medallion (Wrapped.)
  Knitting and needles

ACT II

STRIKE:
  Coffee cups
  Film
  All pictures
  Canapes
  Typewriter
  Bomb
  Gun
  Allison's notepad
  Sabbath candles
  Camera box & wrapping
  1 martini & glass
  Milk carton
  Cake
  Cudites

BEDROOM

Hang Polo shirt on headboard of bed
Remake bed

On Card Table:
   Will
   Computer printout
   Accounts ledger

LIVING ROOM

Ellen's vest (On stage right chair.)
Ellen's bag (On floor next to stage right chair.)
Nancy's purse (Under right end of coffee table.)

On Coffee table:
   2 "dirty" paper plates
   Nancy's steno pad & pen
   Put new pack of film in camera
   Slice of cake on paper plate & fork

Change candle stubs

KITCHEN

On counter:
   Pitcher of milk
   Glass

OFF STAGE UP LEFT *(Kitchen.)*

Put Teapot w/ tea on tea tray
Put bowl of cottage cheese on tea tray

COSTUME PLOT

ELLEN PORTER
    Paisley print skirt
    Turquoise blouse—short sleeve
    Burgundy thigh-length vest
    Leather sandals
    Suntan panty hose
    Wrist watch
    Large shoulder bag

NANCY GRAHAM
    Blue Denim Jeans—flare legs
    Navy blue knit V-neck pullover
    Light brown ankle-high high-heel boots

SUSAN PORTER
    Lavender silk dress
    Nude panty hose
    Bone color high heels
    Pearl necklace
    Engagement & wedding ring

    White apron w/ floral print (Preset in kitchen.)

STEPHEN PORTER
  Light grey slacks
  Purple polo shirt
  Brown leather belt
  Grey socks
  Brown lace-up casual shoes

Preset onstage:
  Pink dress shirt w/ white pin stripes
  Blue & Grey print tie

LARRY PORTER
  Grey flannel trousers
  White cotton dress shirt w/ blue & red checks
  Grey loafers
  Grey socks
  Grey belt

Act I Quick change off stage:
  Cream color dress shirt
  Light blue tie w/ yellow & red stripe
  Blue seersucker jacket

GEORGE ALLISON
  Khaki fatigues — slacks & shirt
  Tan boots

— SCENE DESIGN —
"DOMESTIC ISSUES"

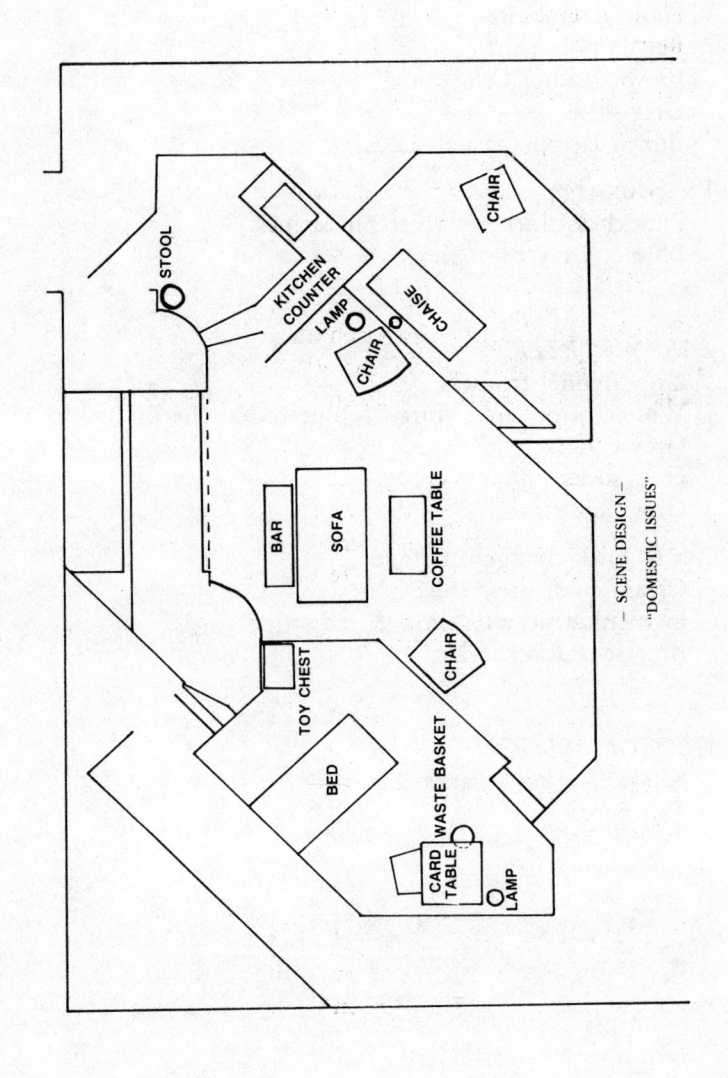

New PLAYS

CHILDREN OF A LESSER GOD
PASSIONE
G. R. POINT
TIME AND GINGER
FATHERS AND SONS
THREE SISTERS
FULL MOON
THE ORPHANS
DUCK HUNTING
THE UBU PLAYS
TENNESSEE
THE COAL DIAMOND
WOMEN STILL WEEP
THE EXHIBITION

DRAMATISTS PLAY SERVICE, INC.
440 Park Avenue South   New York, N. Y. 10016

New
PLAYS

HOME

CLOTHES FOR A SUMMER HOTEL

KID CHAMPION

MARIE AND BRUCE

HIDE AND SEEK

JOSEPHINE: THE MOUSE SINGER

THE GIRLS OF THE GARDEN CLUB

UNCLE VANYA

THE PALACE AT 4 A.M.

SISTER MARY IGNATIUS EXPLAINS IT ALL FOR YOU

BAG LADY

COMPANIONS OF THE FIRE

CINDERELLA WORE COMBAT BOOTS

DRAMATISTS PLAY SERVICE, INC.
440 PARK AVENUE SOUTH   NEW YORK, N.Y. 10016

NEW
Plays

THE LADY FROM DUBUQUE
SALT LAKE CITY SKYLINE
CHARACTER LINES
TWO SMALL BODIES
INNOCENT THOUGHTS,
HARMLESS INTENTIONS
SUMMER BRAVE
A MONTH IN THE COUNTRY
MY COUSIN RACHEL
THE FOLDING GREEN
THIRD AND OAK:
THE LAUNDROMAT
LONE STAR & PVT. WARS
CONVERSATION WITH A SPHINX
FIVE ONE ACT PLAYS
BY MURRAY SCHISGAL

DRAMATISTS PLAY SERVICE, INC.
440 PARK AVENUE SOUTH   NEW YORK, N.Y. 10016

New PLAYS

THE AMERICAN CLOCK
CHILDE BYRON
CLOSE OF PLAY
THE TRADING POST
THE LEGENDARY STARDUST BOYS
CLOSE TIES
OPAL'S MILLION DOLLAR DUCK
IN FIREWORKS LIE SECRET CODES
STOPS ALONG THE WAY
VILLAINOUS COMPANY
THE ACTOR'S NIGHTMARE

Inquiries Invited

DRAMATISTS PLAY SERVICE, INC.
440 Park Avenue South   New York, N. Y. 10016